D1154191

PRACTICAL FISHKEEPING

PUFFERFISH

Chris Ralph

RINGPRESS

DEDICATION

My wife, Kate, for all her help and support. My children, Eleanor, Charlotte and Katherine. My parents, Rosemary and Tom. To the memories of my best friend, Graham Eakins, and those of Adrian Blake and Mervyn Strange.

ACKNOWLEDGEMENTS

Dr Peter Burgess for his inspiration and asking me to write this publication. Giles and Amanda Barlow of Barlows Aquatic Trading, Accrington, Lancashire. BD Aquarium Sand for providing substrate. Raul J. Yallan, Ian and Rhona Walker, Arthur Marshall, David Davis, Nick Wood, Tim Chamberlain, and Robin Warne for their help and support. Sue and Ron Bungay-Perrin, Association of Aquarists, for providing information. Peter & Theresa White for their invaluable support, advice, and proof reading. Julian Dignall for help with the photography. Paul Tapley of Maidenhead Aquatics (Woking), Gareth, Mary and Tony Allen of Porton Aquatic & Pet Centre (Salisbury), Barry of Badshot Lea Garden Centre, Maidenhead Aquatics (Newbury) and the Cichlid Exchange Team – who all provided fish for photographing. Creature Comforts and Aquatic Centre, Southampton, for their help with locating some specimens.

SCIENTIFIC CONSULTANT: Dr. Peter Burgess BSc, MSc, MPhil, PhD is an experienced aquarium hobbyist and international consultant on ornamental fish.

Photography: Chris Ralph (7, 24 – top, 28 – bottom, 32, 37, 40, 62 – bottom, 63), Steve Cranham, Faces Photography (6, 8, 11, 14, 17, 18, 21, 23, 24, 25, 28, 29 – top two, 34, 35, 38, 42, 43, 44, 46, 47, 48, 50, 51, 52, 53, 60 – bottom, 62 – top, 64 – top) and Keith Allison (4, 9, 10, 26, 55, 57, 60, 64 – bottom).

Picture editor: Claire Horton-Bussey **Design:** *Rob Benson*

Published by Ringpress Books,
a division of Interpet Publishing,
Vincent Lane, Dorking, Surrey, RH4 3YX, UK
Tel: 01306 873822   Fax: 01306 876712

email: sales@interpet.co.uk

First published 2003 by Ringpress Books. All rights reserved
No part of this book may be reproduced or transmitted in any form or by any means, electronic or mechanical, including photocopying, recording, or by any information storage and retrieval system, without permission in writing from the publisher.

ISBN 1 86054 2 336

Printed and bound in Hong Kong through Printworks International Ltd.
10 9 8 7 6 5 4 3 2 1

CONTENTS

WHAT IS A PUFFERFISH?

Puffers are unique fish, each with their own individual characters – and this probably explains why most people actually name their pet Puffers. They are best known for their ability to puff themselves up into balls (hence the name, of course), but, as owners will testify, there is much, much more to Pufferfish than their puff!

PUFFER ANATOMY

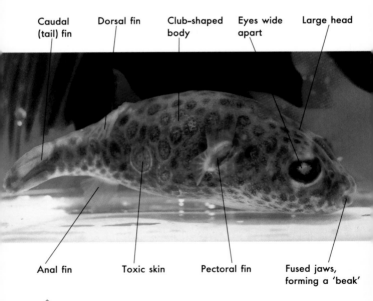

Caudal (tail) fin

Dorsal fin

Club-shaped body

Eyes wide apart

Large head

Anal fin

Toxic skin

Pectoral fin

Fused jaws, forming a 'beak'

BODY AND HEAD

A typical Pufferfish is club-shaped, which consequently gives them a rather clumsy appearance. The head is generally large in comparison with the rest of a Puffer's body, and the eyes are very widely separated, so that they can look out for prey (Puffers do not have many predators because their skin contains toxins – page 8).

FINS

These are anatomically and functionally different to those of 'typical' fish. For example, in most other varieties of fish, the caudal fin (tail) forms the main organ of propulsion, while the paired fins act as the mechanism by which the fish steers itself.

In Puffers, this situation is quite the opposite. The body is driven along by the screw-like movements of the powerful pectoral fins with assistance from the dorsal and anal fins, while the tail does the steering. The pectoral fins can work independently and so can determine the direction of movement without the help of the vertical fins.

MOVEMENT

The specialised muscles of the pectoral fins also make it possible for these fish to swim backwards. These varied movements give Puffers a much greater manoeuvrability than their clumsy appearance would suggest.

SKIN

A Puffer's fins are composed only of soft rays. Their skin is naked – in other words it is devoid of scales – but it is lined with small bony plates or spines, known as dermal spines.

TEETH/JAWS

The Tetraodontidae belong to the order Tetrao-
dontiformes (Plectognathi), or 'fused jawed ones', which
encompasses all Pufferfish. They have four teeth or teeth
plates – two in the upper mandible and two in the lower
mandible. The teeth are fused together in their
respective pairs (i.e. upper and lower), thereby forming
a 'beak', which, in the case of the larger species, such as
Tetraodon mbu (Giant Puffer) or *Tetraodon fahaka* (Nile
Puffer), can give a dangerous nip.

The upper beak is not dissimilar to the shape of a
parrot's beak. Both the upper and lower mandibles of
the beak are each made up of right and left tooth plates.
There are a total of four tooth plates, hence the name
Tetraodontidae or 'four toothed ones'. The mandibles of
Pufferfish are covered by swollen lips.

DENTISTRY

If a Puffer's beak is left to become overgrown, it can
make it difficult for the fish to eat. It is therefore very

The Puffer's jaws form a parrot-like beak.

The beak (teeth) can give a dangerous bite, particularly in large species, such as the Giant Puffer (*Tetraodon mbu*).

important to feed captive Puffers on aquatic snails and cockles, complete with shells, to keep their beaks worn down.

In some cases, it has been known for aquarists to trim overgrown teeth with nail clippers, but this should only ever be done by an experienced person. A fish specialist or vet should be consulted to perform the procedure, or to show you what to do.

SELF-INFLATION

The members of the family Tetraodontidae are also referred to as 'Swell Fishes' or 'Globe Fishes'. This is because Pufferfish are able to inflate themselves with air or water into a veritable balloon. No other group of fish has this remarkable ability.

Puffers have a number of sacs within the oesophagus, which are capable of inflating with water or air to an enormous size. With the aid of these sacs, the fish can inflate themselves into a round shape, an adaptation that probably serves mainly as a means of defence.

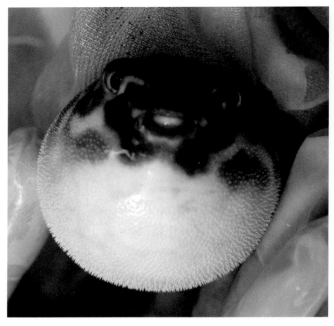

Also known as Swell Fishes or Globe Fishes, Pufferfish are best known for inflating themselves with air or water.

With its greatly increased size, the inflated Puffer probably deters would-be predators by becoming too large to swallow. As a further deterrent, Puffers have spines on their bodies, which become erect when the fish swells up. Potential attackers may be further intimidated by the Puffer's ability to expel water to move itself backwards.

INTOXICATING MIXTURE

Many Puffers possess toxins in their body tissues, and, like other groups of animals in nature, advertise this fact by their bright warning coloration.

Various nerve toxins (neurotoxins) are produced and include tetrodotoxin (also known as tarichatoxin and tetragorin), which is produced in the gonads of the fish and is subsequently stored in various other organs in the body. These neurotoxins are secreted when the fish becomes stressed and they are able to produce fatal cardiorespiratory effects on nearby fish. The liver and ovaries are the most toxic parts of these fish.

Pufferfish extracts have been used in witchcraft in the Caribbean, inducing an intoxicating trance.

Many Puffers have toxic skin, and advertise this fact in their bright colour pattern.

Puffers are fascinating fish but require specialist care. This Dwarf Puffer needs at least two feeds a day, but has not been fed correctly. It is emaciated and has clamped fins.

FASCINATING FISH

Although Puffers appear to be clumsy, they are extremely active, hardly ever still for a moment, and, as such they are fascinating to watch and keep. However, they are not ideally suited to life in a community aquarium, and are generally extremely territorial and aggressive towards their own kind. (There are always exceptions to this, such as the Spotted Congo Puffer, *Tetraodon schoutedeni*, which is quite happy to be kept with other members of the same species – see pages 28-30.)

The other consideration before committing yourself to caring for Pufferfish is that they are complex fish, and so are not ideal for the novice fishkeeper. However, given the right conditions, they make excellent pets.

CHAPTER 2

A PUFFERFISH HOME

Pufferfish can be split into three categories: those that require a freshwater aquarium, those that require a brackish (slightly salty) one, and finally of course, marine Puffers, not covered here. Which fish is suited to which set-up will depend on the fish's place of origin, and you should research each fish's specific needs before bringing it home.

WATER CONDITIONS

There are several factors that will differ according to whether you are caring for a freshwater or brackish species, including temperature, hardness and pH.

Pufferfish are divided into freshwater and brackish species, each with its own specific requirements. Pictured: adolescent Nile Puffer (*Tetraodon lineatus*), a freshwater fish.

Water hardness is a measure of the amount of certain dissolved salts present in the water. This publication refers to total or general hardness values, which are related to the levels of calcium or magnesium present in the water. Soft water is said to have a hardness value below 8°GH; Moderately hard water is around 8 to 18°GH; Hard water above 18°GH.

The pH of water is an indication of the degree of acidity or alkalinity, based on a logarithmic scale. Chemically speaking, the pH scale is based on the concentration of hydrogen ions present in the water.

FRESH VERSUS BRACKISH
The ideal conditions required for freshwater and brackish water species of Puffers are as follows:

Freshwater
- Hardness in the range of 5 to 20°GH
- pH in the range of 5.8 to 8.0
- Temperature in the range of 22 to 28°C (72 to 82°F).

Brackish
- Hardness of 10°GH
- pH 7.6 to 8.1
- Temperature in the range of 23 to 28°C (73 to 82°F).

These are only approximate ranges; optimal conditions will depend on the species of Pufferfish (see Chapter Five).

The more hydrogen ions present, the more acid the
water and subsequently the pH value is lower. The scale
ranges from 0 being extremely acidic, to 14 being
extremely alkaline, with pH7 being neutral.

Most good aquatic retailers offer test kits for sale, or,
for a small fee, may even test the water for you.

FRESHWATER AQUARIUM

Several Puffer species are suited to freshwater
aquariums. In the wild, freshwater Puffers, unlike the
brackish species, do not have to tolerate wide extremes
of water chemistry (e.g. salinity); in other words, they
are accustomed to fairly constant water conditions.

Specific details, such as the size of the aquarium and
water temperature, will be given for each of the species
covered in Chapter Five. Typical aquarium materials
and equipment required for keeping freshwater Puffers
are as follows:

- Fine gravel or good-quality aquarium sand as a
  substrate.
- Rocks, including Tufa rock, pebbles, sandstone etc.
  It is very important when choosing rocks as décor
  and for providing hiding places, that they are suitable
  for aquarium use, i.e. they do not contain traces of
  cement on their surfaces or any other impurities that
  could harm the fish.
- Bogwood. This helps to provide cover and security to
  the fish, and helps to decorate the aquarium. There
  are possible risks to consider if using other woods –
  they may contain toxic substances or introduce
  disease or parasites.
- Aquatic plants (see pages 16 and 19).

FRESHWATER SET-UPS

Provided the basic 'rules' of a freshwater aquarium are followed, many different looks can be created.

◀ Tufa rock (left), *Anubias* sp. on bogwood (centre), and Java fern on bogwood (right).

Barnacle clusters ▶ (left), shells (foreground), and Tufa rock (right).

- Sufficient lighting to maintain plant growth. To promote plant growth, lighting should ideally be provided for approximately 12 hours per day. Longer lighting periods may result in unsightly algal growth. Most aquaria will suffice with a single fluorescent light. For example, a 36 x 15 x 12 in (90 x 38 x 30 cm) aquarium will require a single 30 in (75 cm) 25 watt fluorescent tube. Some aquatic plants will need more intense lighting. For those plant species mentioned in this book, single tubes should be sufficient.

- Good-quality internal or external filtration dependent upon the size of the aquarium and the species of Puffer to be kept. The Puffer supplier or store should be able to advise the customer. If power filtration is not available, then suitable air-driven filtration should be provided in the form of corner box filters and bubble-up sponge filters, which are suitable for some of the smaller species only. Due to the fact that sand and/or fine gravel have been suggested here as suitable substrates, undergravel filtration would not be recommended for these fish as it will tend to become clogged.
- A good-quality heater-thermostat.
- An aquarium thermometer to monitor that the correct temperature is being maintained, according to the species kept (see Chapter Five). Choose either a digital one or a glass variety that sticks to the inside of the tank.

BRACKISH AQUARIUM

Brackish water habitats lie somewhere between freshwater and marine environments in terms of their salt content. Pure freshwater has a specific gravity (or SG) of 1.000, while seawater has a specific gravity of around 1.025, depending upon the particular sea or ocean in question and the temperature. Brackish water, however, does not correspond to an exact specific gravity value, although a figure between 1.005 and 1.015 is regarded as brackish.

Seawater contains approximately 35 grammes of sea salt per litre (1.2 oz per 2 pints) of water. In order to create brackish water, it is best to make up full-strength seawater and dilute it with tapwater. For example, mix

FRESHWATER PLANT LIFE

There are many aquatic plant species that are suitable for the freshwater Puffer aquarium.

- Anubias *(Anubias barteri* or *Anubias nana)*
- Aponogeton *(Aponogeton crispus)*
- Canadian Pondweed *(Elodea canadensis)*
- Crypto *(Cryptocoryne* spp.*)*
- Dwarf Hygrophila *(Hygrophila polysperma)*
- Floating Plants, such as Water Lettuce *(Pistia* spp.*)* and Riccia *(Riccia* spp.*)*
- Hornwort *(Ceratophyllum* spp.*)*
- Indian Fern *(Ceratopteris cornuta)*
- Java Fern *(Microsorium* spp.*)*
- Java Moss *(Vesicularia dubyana)*
- Swordplants *(Echinodorus* spp.*)*
- Vallis *(Vallisneria spiralis)*

Cryptcoryne sp.

Indian Fern.

Water lettuce
(*Pistia stratiotes*).

Amazon sword
(*Echinodorus* sp.)

one part seawater to one part fresh, which would give a specific gravity of about 1.012. You can test the salinity by using a hydrometer (see page 20).

The fish that are able to survive in these environments are those that can tolerate fluctuations in salinity and temperature – one example being *Tetraodon fluviatilis*, known as the Green Puffer (page 46).

The Green Puffer (*Tetraodon fluviatilis*) is one of several species that is best kept in a brackish-water aquarium.

SALTY SET-UP

There are two typical brackish aquarium set-ups, namely the mangrove swamp and the typical aquarium appearance. The choice of layout is obviously down to individual taste and preferences. As those Puffers referred to in this publication (with the exception of the truly marine species) are to be found naturally occurring in estuaries (with fluctuating salinities), then it would perhaps be most appropriate to choose a mangrove swamp layout.

Typical materials required for this style of layout would include the following items:

BRACKISH SET-UPS

There are two types of brackish tanks that can be created, according to the fish that are kept and to personal preferences.

A brackish aquarium: created using different-coloured Tufa rock, Java fern, and Java moss.

The mangrove swamp: created by using bogwood to depict mangrove roots, and Java fern.

- Good-quality aquarium sand as a substrate. Fine gravel can be used if sand is not available.
- Tufa rock (see page 13).
- Bogwood, ideally pieces which have the appearance of tree roots, which could then be positioned to look as if the roots were entering the water from the surface (see also page 13).

SALT-TOLERANT PLANT SPECIES

Here are a few species that are suitable for a brackish aquarium.

- Canadian Pondweed *(Elodea canadensis)*
- Dwarf Hygrophila *(Hygrophila polysperma)*
- Hornwort *(Ceratophyllum spp.)*
- Java Fern *(Microsorium pteropus)*
- Java Moss *(Vesicularia dubyana)*
- Sagittaria *(Sagittaria spp.)*
- Swordplants *(Echinodorus spp.)*
- Vallis *(Vallisneria spiralis).*

Dwarf hygrophila.

Echinodorus sp.

Vallisneria sp.

Java fern (*Microsorium pteropus*).

- Salt-tolerant species of aquatic plants (see page 19).
- A good-quality internal or external filter, dependent on the size of the aquarium, or box-type filtration if air-driven. As with the freshwater aquarium, undergravel filtration is not advised because the fine substrate may clog it.
- A good-quality heater-thermostat.
- Thermometer, as per the freshwater set-up (see page 15).
- Sufficient lights for the aquarium size and to promote plant growth (see page 14).
- Hydrometer to check salinity. Ideally choose a model that reads down to 1.000 (many don't).

CARING FOR PUFFERS

Unlike a general community aquarium, you will be maintaining a smaller number of fish in a Puffer aquarium. If looked after correctly, the fish will be fairly easy to maintain.

FEEDING AND NUTRITION

It is essential to offer a mixed and varied diet to captive Puffers in order for them to survive and remain healthy. Some species of Puffers are mostly carnivorous (meat-eaters) while others are omnivorous, eating meat and plant foods. The species profiles in Chapter Five describe each fish's diet.

Pufferfish require a varied diet. Pictured: Dwarf Puffer (*Carinotetraodon travancoricus*) feeding on bloodworm.

CARNIVORE PUFFERS

Typical foods for the carnivorous Puffers include:

- Aquatic snails
- Chopped and whole mussel
- Chopped liver in bite-sized pieces, which must be fed very sparingly so as not to pollute the aquarium. Excess animal meat can be harmful to fish
- Earthworms
- Flies
- Live and frozen foods, such as bloodworm, mosquito larvae, *Daphnia*, *Gammarus* (Freshwater shrimps), Glassworm, *Artemia*, *Cyclops*, *Tubifex* and pieces of fish
- Shellfish, such as cockles (complete with shell to keep the Puffers' beaks worn down)
- Whole prawns.

OMNIVORE PUFFERS

Typical foods for the omnivorous Puffers include those for the carnivore diet (above), together with the following items:

- Aquatic plants
- Courgette
- Lettuce
- Peas
- Sinking catfish pellets (once the fish have become acclimatized)
- Tablet foods (once the fish have become acclimatised).

Omnivorous Puffers will eat a selection of foods from both of the above lists, although the actual types of food selected may alter in some species as the Puffer grows. Not all species of Puffer will eat exactly the same foods.

CARNIVORE DIET

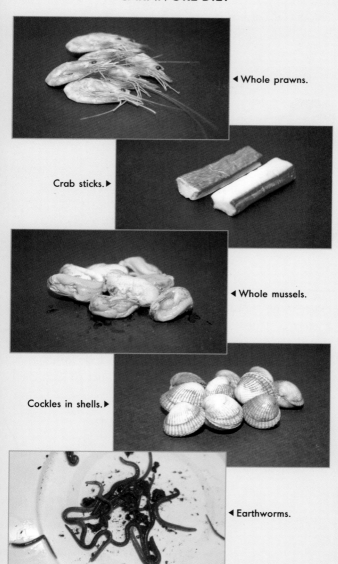

◄ Whole prawns.

Crab sticks. ▶

◄ Whole mussels.

Cockles in shells. ▶

◄ Earthworms.

OMNIVORE DIET

◄ Aquatic plants. This *Anubias nana* has been nibbled by a Figure of Eight Puffer (*Tetraodon biocellatus*).

Sinking catfish pellets. ►

In some cases, the owner of the fish has to experiment in order to establish which foods are preferred. This said, it is still important to offer a mixed diet to prevent the fish from becoming too fussy.

Remember, it is very important to include foods which the Puffer has to crunch on in order to keep the teeth in trim.

A mixed diet will promote health and should prevent the fish becoming too choosy. Pictured Giant Puffer (*Tetradon mbu*)

Commercially-prepared flake food should never form the major part of the diet.

FEEDING REGIMES

Ideally, Puffers should be fed twice daily on fairly small amounts of food. If overfed, Puffers have been known to regurgitate partially-digested food, which can subsequently result in the deterioration of the water quality within the aquarium. If uneaten or ejected food remains in the aquarium for a period of time, it could result in the ill-health – or even death – of the fish.

SAFETY WARNING

When handling any Pufferfish, it is probably wise to wear disposable gloves, as some species have poisonous skins. It is therefore very important to wash your hands immediately after handling these fish.

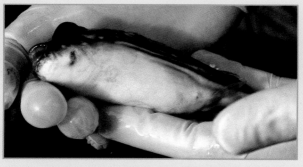

Some Puffers have poisonous skins, so protective gloves should be worn when handling them.

Commercially-prepared foods (e.g. pellet food) should be offered as part of a varied and balanced diet for Puffers, as these foods contain all the essential vitamins and trace elements that captive fish require to maintain good health.

CLEANING AND MAINTENANCE

When keeping Puffers under aquarium conditions, regular, partial water changes should be undertaken to keep the fish and the aquarium healthy.

The extent to which water changes should be carried out really depends upon the species of fish being kept, as well as stocking levels, aquarium size and filtration. A filter will provide the biological mechanism in which waste products will be broken down, but regular, partial water changes are still essential. As a general guide, at least 25 per cent of the aquarium water should be changed on a fortnightly basis.

Even crystal-clear water can contain deadly amounts of ammonia, so test the water regularly and make frequent, partial water changes. Pictured: Palembang Puffer (*Tetraodon palembangensis*).

If replacing the water with tap water, a suitable water conditioner should be added in order to neutralise chlorine and chloramines (although some brands are not very effective at removing more harmful chloramines).

When cleaning the filter media, care must be taken to ensure that it is cleaned in the old aquarium water – siphon some aquarium water into a clean bucket and clean the filter media in this water.

If the filter material is washed out under a tap, the filter's beneficial bacteria – required to maintain the aquarium's biological balance – will be lost, as chlorine acts as a bactericide.

ADDING NEW FISH

When adding newly-purchased stock to an aquarium, it is important to float the fish, within the polythene bag, on the surface of the aquarium water (switch off the aquarium lights). The bag should be floated for between 15 and 20 minutes in order for the water temperature in the bag to equalise to that of the aquarium. Some aquarists prefer to open the bag and gradually introduce water from the aquarium into the bag to get the fish acclimatised. Once floated, the Puffer can be released into the aquarium. Newly-introduced stock can initially appear shy and retiring until they have settled into their new surroundings.

Most Puffers can be territorial towards their own kind or other fish when kept in a community aquarium environment. It is essential that the aquarist observes the newly-purchased stock to check that it has settled in and that there are no problems with the other fish that may be kept with it.

New fish should always be quarantined. Pictured: juvenile Nile Puffer (*Tetraodon lineatus*).

If the aquarist has researched his or her purchase correctly, there should not be too many problems with adding the Puffers to an established aquarium.

Ideally, all newly-purchased stock should be quarantined in a separate aquarium for a minimum of two weeks, but preferably for three weeks.

TANKMATES FOR FRESHWATER PUFFERS

Because most of the Puffer species described in this publication can be quite aggressive, any companions for a Puffer aquarium must be large enough to withstand any quarrels, such as:

• Larger South American Armoured Catfish (such as *Hoplosternum* sp.) and Bubblenest Catfishes (*Megalechis personata, Hoplosternum littorale*)
• African Synodontis Catfishes (*Synodontis nigrita*)
• Larger Barbs (*Barbodes schwanenfeldi*)
• Anabantids, such as the Kissing Gourami (*Helostoma temminckii*).

Generally, if you are keeping, or are thinking of keeping, Puffers, it is best to keep the larger species as single specimens, while some of the smaller species can

SUITABLE TANKMATES FOR FRESHWATER PUFFERS

Most Puffers are territorial and can be quarrelsome. The following tankmates are large enough to stand their own!

Bubblenest Catfish (*Megalechis thoracata*).

Pink Kissing Gourami (*Helostoma temminckii*).

Ornate Bagrid (*Amarginops ornatus*).

be kept together in species-only tanks. There are perhaps a couple of species that may tolerate being kept together, such as *Tetraodon nigroviridis* and *Tetraodon schoutedeni*. In most cases, however, it is probably best to maintain species-only aquariums to avoid any possible conflicts.

HEALTH PROBLEMS

As with all livestock, it is important that the owner ensures that good hygiene is maintained at all times.

WHITESPOT

Perhaps the most common ailment with freshwater Puffers is Whitespot or Ich (*Ichthyophthirius*), a highly infectious disease sometimes triggered by stress. It is important to make sure that fish you buy have been quarantined by the dealer, as the shock of being transported can trigger the disease.

Fortunately, this disease is easily treated with proprietary anti-whitespot medications, which are available in liquid form from aquarium stores.

FUNGUS (*SAPROLEGNIA*)

This is another disease that Puffers can suffer from. A fungal infection may be as the result of an open wound caused by another fish, or, most likely, a conspecific (member of the same species) attacking or biting the affected fish.

Fungus (and other infections) may also result from the fish getting too close to an aquarium heater and burning itself. In order to overcome this problem, heater guards can be purchased from most good aquatic retailers.

Imported fish may carry flukes, so should always be quarantined and treated where necessary.
Pictured: gill fluke.

As with Whitespot, fungal infections are relatively easy to treat, using a proprietary brand of medication available from aquatic retailers.

FLUKES

When Puffers are imported from their natural habitat, flukes may be present. Flukes fall into two categories: gill flukes and skin flukes.

- **Gill flukes (*Dactylogyrus*).** They are difficult to see without the aid of a magnifying glass or microscope. Affected fish may appear listless and may spend a lot of time near sources of aeration (e.g. air stones).
- **Skin flukes (*Gyrodactylus*).** These flukes live on the skin of the fish and may cause the fish to flick.

Both types can be treated with proprietary aquarium medications.

FIN ROT

This can be caused by other fish fin-nipping or damage caused by careless netting or handling. Poor water will increase the risks of fin rot – therefore it is important to maintain good water quality at all times. Proprietary aquarium treatments will help to speed up recovery from fin rot. For further information, consult *Common Fish Ailments* by Dr Peter Burgess in this *Practical Fishkeeping* series.

CHAPTER

4

BREEDING PUFFERFISH

There are a small number of freshwater and brackish Puffers that have been successfully spawned in an aquarium to date. There are various reasons why Puffers may be reluctant breeders:

- There is little information about the breeding requirements of some species.
- There are no obvious external sexual differences, and so identifying a suitable breeding pair may be difficult.

Breeding can be restricted by the fish's size. The Giant Puffer (*Tetraodon mbu*), for example, requires a large tank to breed.

- Incompatibility of conspecifics – i.e. some Puffers may not tolerate one another in their natural environment, and males and females may only come together to breed.
- The size of the aquarium may be inadequate. Some species, such as the Mbu Puffer, require a large volume of water in which to breed.
- The actual cost of purchasing potential breeding stock can also be inhibiting to some fishkeepers.

It is hoped that, as more information regarding this fascinating group of fish becomes available, more aquarists will take up the challenge to breed these fish and hopefully document their successes as well as their failures.

Raising the fry from a successful spawning poses the greatest challenge to the fishkeeper, as Puffer fry require very small foods initially, which can be a problem. Most successful Puffer breeders have had some success with small starter foods, such as infusoria and *Cyclops*, before continuing with newly-hatched brine shrimp, and gradually progressing on to larger foods as the fry grow.

SPAWNING VARIETIES
Pufferfish basically fall into one of three types:

SUBSTRATE SPAWNERS
These fish dig pits in the substrate into which the eggs are deposited. They protect their eggs and guard the fry against predators.

Substrate-spawning Puffers include the Green Puffer (*Tetraodon fluviatilis*) and the Twin Spot Puffer (*Tetraodon leiurus brevirostris*).

The male Green Puffer (*Tetraodon fluviatilis*) guards the eggs.

The Green Puffer excavates or digs pits in the substrate into which the eggs are deposited and subsequently guarded. It is widely documented that the male fish take on the role of guarding the eggs and fry from would-be predators. It is important to note that the Green Puffer has only been successfully bred when kept in brackish water, even though this particular species can be found in both fresh and brackish waters in the wild.

The Twin Spot Puffer is another substrate spawner. When in breeding condition, the female appears more rounded in the body, which is a good sign that she is full of eggs and ready to spawn with her partner. Once the eggs have been deposited in the pit and the male has fertilised them, he then chases the female away and guards the 'nest'.

A single spawning could result in up to 500 eggs, which are clear in appearance. It is reported that the eggs take up to five days to hatch. The fry should be fed on *Artemia* (newly-hatched brine shrimp) and *Cyclops*.

Once the fry are free-swimming, the parent fish should be removed to a separate tank. The fry can be introduced into an adult tank when they have reached a large enough size not to be eaten.

When raising any young fish, it is inevitable that some will be lost due to weakness, overcrowding, or from being eaten by their siblings. Out of a brood of 500 fish, it would be realistic to raise between 25 and 30 fish. Do bear in mind that, as they grow, they may have to be separated if they become territorial towards each other. The excess stock could be given to other aquarists to grow on.

ROCK/STONE SPAWNERS

These fish lay their eggs on the surface of a rock or flat stone. They usually offer some parental care to the eggs and subsequent fry, as no real shelter from would-be predators is provided. Rock or stone spawning species include the Sea Frog (*Tetraodon cutcutia*) and the Spotted Green Puffer (*Tetraodon nigroviridis*).

The Sea Frog requires a large aquarium in which to spawn, up to 72 in (length) x 18 in x 18 in (180 cm x 45 cm x 45 cm), and this is mainly due to the quarrelsome nature of the adult fish. When ready to breed, the edge of the male's caudal fin turns red and he displays himself to the female by 'dancing' in front of her.

The Sea Frog (*Tetraodon cutcutia*) spawns on rocks or flat stones.

The eggs are deposited on flat stones that have previously been 'cleaned' by the mating pair – they do this by rubbing their bodies over the surface of the rock and using their teeth to remove any algae or debris built up on the stone. Once laid, the eggs are subsequently guarded by the male.

The eggs can take up to 10 days to hatch, according to the water temperature. After the fry have emerged from the eggs, the male should be removed from the tank to prevent him from eating the fry.

Initially, foods offered to the fry should include *Cyclops* and newly-hatched brine shrimp (*Artemia*). As the fry grow, larger-sized foods can be offered, such as *Daphnia* and bloodworm, until eventually they will eat cockles, prawns and mussels.

The Spotted Green Puffer's breeding behaviour is very similar – they spawn their eggs on the surface of a clean rock, and the males guard the eggs and subsequent fry from being attacked by predators.

PLANT SPAWNERS

These fish lay their eggs among the leaves or roots of an aquatic plant. They care for the eggs and fry in the early stages of development by hiding them in aquatic plants, thus providing limited shelter from potential predators.

Plant spawning species include the Figure of Eight Puffer (*Tetraodon biocellatus*), the Spotted Congo Puffer (*Tetraodon schoutedeni*), and the Red Eye Puffer (*Carinotetraodon lorteti*).

The Figure of Eight Puffer tends to lay its pale-coloured, glassy eggs among aquatic plant leaves. Once they have been laid, the female is chased away and the

The Figure of Eight Puffer (*Tetraodon biocellatus*) spawns among aquatic plants.

male guards the eggs until they hatch, which can take six or seven days. As with the other species, small foods are required initially to raise the fry.

The Spotted Congo Puffer also deposits its eggs among plant leaves. During courtship, the male grasps the female's stomach with his mouth, and, as she deposits the eggs on the plants, he fertilises them. As with most other species, the male guards the eggs and subsequent fry.

The Red Eye Puffer spawns up to 350 eggs among clumps of Java Moss. During courtship and the act of spawning, the male holds the female in his jaws. Unusually, both parents should be removed after spawning, as they will eat the eggs if given the opportunity. The eggs hatch after 30 hours. As with the other species, small foods should be fed to the fry or they will perish due to starvation.

REARING FRY

Mostly, eggs are clear or pale-coloured and can number up to 500 in a single spawning. Hatching time varies according to the species, which can be up to ten days or as short as 30 hours.

In the interests of the eggs' safety, the male (bottom) and female (top) Red Eye Puffer (*Carinotetraodon lorteti*) should be removed after spawni

When attempting to raise fry, it is important to appreciate that these fish are very small, and therefore require suitably-sized first foods, such as *Cyclops* and *Artemia*, if they are to stand any chance of surviving. There are commercially-available liquid and powdered fry foods, which could also be considered when feeding the young fry, although these may not be as successful.

It is also important to take account of water quality at all times. If the aquarium water is polluted due to over feeding, this will result in the loss of fry. One should always practise good aquarium husbandry and carry out regular, partial water changes to give the fry the best possible chances of survival. Of course, this practice also applies when keeping the adult brood stock as well.

CHAPTER 5

PUFFER SPECIES

This chapter contains descriptions of the most popular – or unusual – species of Puffer. Under the heading for each Puffer, there is a measurement given in mm standard length (SL). Standard length is the measurement of a fish taken from the tip of the snout to the base of the caudal peduncle; in other words, the size measurement does not include the length of the tail.

> ### DÉCOR
> **Unless otherwise noted, all the fish in this chapter should be provided with a heavily-planted aquarium, with an open swimming space and hiding places amongst bogwood, an upturned, clean, eathenware flower pot and/or rocks (see Chapter Two).**

FIGURE OF EIGHT PUFFER

Also known as: Eyespot Puffer.
Scientific name: *Tetraodon biocellatus.*
Synonyms: *Chelonodon biocellatus, Tetraodon steindachneri.*
Size: 6 cm (2 ³/₈ in).

Identifying characteristics: the upper side of the body is lemon yellow to deep green, with the underside

The Figure of Eight Puffer (*Tetraodon biocellatus*) is an aggressive fish that should only be kept with its own species.

white or yellow. On the flanks and upper part of the body, there can be seen an irregular pattern of lines and black blotches. The skin is covered with prominent dermal spines.

These fish posses an ocellus ('eye-spot') under the dorsal fin and one on the caudal peduncle, which are black with a pale border. There is also a large black blotch on the shoulder.

The pupils are dark-coloured and the irises, gold. The nostrils have smooth inner surfaces.

There are 10 to 14 dorsal fin rays, and 11 to 12 anal fin rays.

Natural habitat: south-east Asia, Sumatra, Borneo, Malaysian peninsula and Thailand. Naturally found in slow-flowing or standing freshwater habitats.

Housing: minimum aquarium size: 30 x 15 x 12 in (75 x 38 x 30 cm).

Water: good-quality, clean freshwater is required with

soft to medium hardness (between 5 and 12°GH and pH 7.0). The ideal temperature range is 22 to 26°C (72 to 79°F).

Diet: carnivorous (see pages 22-23). This species will occasionally feed on the scales and fins of other fish. Plant material is eaten occasionally, including lettuce.

Sexual differences: there are no known external sexual differences.

Breeding: the male guards the pale-coloured, glassy eggs after they have been laid on plant leaves. The eggs hatch after six to seven days.

Remarks: an active but aggressive fish, which should ideally be kept in a species-only aquarium. The Figure of Eight Puffer occupies the mid to bottom areas of an aquarium.

SEA FROG

Also known as: Ocellated Puffer, or Emerald Puffer.
Scientific name: *Tetraodon cutcutia*.
Synonyms: *Tetrodon cutcutia, Tetrodon caria, Tetrodon gularis, Leisomus cutcutia, Leisomus marmoratus, Monotretus cutcutia, Monotreta gularis*.
Size: 150 mm (6 in).

Identifying characteristics: the body is olive green/dark green in the upper region or back of the body, with a whitish/cream coloration to the lower half of the body. The upper body half is patterned with emerald-green, sandy, and dark patches. The fins are yellow/grey to olive green. The outer edge of the caudal

The Sea Frog Pufferfish (*Tetraodon cutcutia*), is found in ponds, rivers, and canals.

fin can be red. The body lacks dermal spines, and the skin is leathery.

The eyes have dark, greenish pupils, with a red or dark iris. The nostril openings form a short tube with a single opening, and there are 10 to 12 dorsal fin rays, 10 anal fin rays, and 21 pectoral fin rays.

Natural habitat: Asia, Sri Lanka, Bangladesh, the Indian states of Assam, Bengal and Orissa. Found naturally in ponds, rivers and canals.

Housing: minimum aquarium size 36 x 15 x 12 in (90 x 38 x 30 cm). They prefer an aquarium with aquatic plants in the background and arranged at the sides, and require open swimming spaces, with hiding places.

Water: medium to hard water conditions are required with 10°GH and over, and neutral pH 7.0. The ideal temperature range is 24 to 28°C (74 to 82°F).

Diet: omnivorous (see pages 22-24). When acclimatised, tablet foods and some vegetables, such as peas and courgette, may also be accepted.

Sexual differences: the males are said to have nuptial coloration (described below); the females tend to be smaller with lighter yellow coloration.

Breeding: this species has been successfully bred in captivity, and requires a large aquarium of around 60 x 18 x 18 in (150 x 45 x 45) or 72 x 24 x 24 in (180 x 60 x 60 cm) due to the quarrelsome nature of the adult Puffers.

When in breeding condition, the edge of the caudal fin of the male fish has red coloration and he displays to the female by 'dancing' in front of her.

The eggs are deposited on clean, flat stones and are subsequently guarded by the male. Hatching of the eggs takes between six and ten days, depending upon the water temperature.

Once the eggs have hatched, the male should be removed to prevent him from eating the resultant fry. The fry require very small foods e.g. *Cyclops* during the initial stages of rearing, which can present problems with growing them on. It has been suggested that, when kept in groups, the males will practise brood care.

The Sea Frog Puffer has been bred in captivity, but requires a large tank to be successful.

Remarks: adult specimens tend to be quarrelsome towards each other, while juveniles tend to be more tolerant of each other. It is therefore recommended that single specimens be kept, unless space is available to keep several similar-sized fish together. This species occupies all ranges of the aquarium.

If removed from the water, these fish inflate themselves into a sphere shape and make quacking, croaking noises (perhaps this is why the inhabitants of Malabar, India, call it the 'Sea Frog').

NILE PUFFER

Also known as: Coral Butterfly, Arab Puffer, Fahaka Puffer.

Scientific name: *Tetraodon lineatus*.

Synonyms: *Tetraodon fahaka fahaka, Tetraodon lineatus, Tetraodon lineatus lineatus, Tetraodon lineatum, Tetraodon physa, Tetraodon fahaka strigosus, Tetraodon fahaka rudolfianus, Tetraodon lineatus rudolfianus, Crayracion fahaca, Tetrodon fahaka, Tetrodon lineatus, Tetrodon physa, Tetrodon strigosus.*

The Nile Puffer (*Tetraodon lineatus*).

Size: 450 mm (18 in).

Identifying characteristics: The upper half of the body is dark grey to black, and the underside is yellow. The flanks (sides) of the body are grey/yellow, with a number of dark, longitudinal bands that are inclined slightly upwards, forming a marbled pattern.

Juvenile fish display this marbled pattern in the form of rows and blotches, and may have rows of spots on their flanks.

The dorsal, anal and pectoral fins are yellow. The caudal fin is dark grey to olive, with an outer border of orange. The fin ray count is 12 to 14 dorsal fin rays and 10 to 11 anal fin rays.

The eyes have dark-coloured pupils with a yellow to gold iris, and the nostrils are short and forked. There are small dermal spines on the head and body.

Natural habitat: the freshwaters of Africa: Senegal, Gambia, Volta, Niger, Geba, Chad basin, Nile and Lake Rudolf. These Pufferfish are naturally found in large rivers, open water, reed beds and the vegetated fringes of rivers.

Housing: minimum aquarium size: 48 x 18 x 18 in (120 x 45 x 45 cm), although 72 x 24 x 24 in (180 x 60 x 60 cm) would be preferable.

Water: medium to hard neutral water conditions are required with 10°GH and pH 7.0. The ideal temperature range for the Nile Puffer is between 24 to 26°C (75 to 79°F).

Diet: carnivorous (see pages 22-23).

The male Nile Puffer is more colourful than the female.
Pictured: a juvenile male.

Sexual differences: adult males are said to be more colourful and larger than the females.

Breeding: no known records of breeding in captivity. Due to the size, which these fishes attain, spawning in an average-sized aquarium is highly unlikely due to the amount of space that would be required.

Remarks: while this is perhaps one of the hardiest species, the Nile Puffer should be kept in a species-only aquarium due to its aggressive behaviour, and more than one specimen should not be kept in close confines.

This fish likes to bury itself in the sand, leaving its eyes protruding from the substrate, while it waits to ambush any passing prey. This Puffer occupies the mid to bottom ranges of the aquarium.

GREEN PUFFER

Also known as: Tidal Puffer.
Scientific name: *Tetraodon fluviatilis.*
Synonyms: *Tetrodon fluviatilis, Tetrodon nigroviridis, Tetrodon simulans, Arothron dorsovittatus, Arothron simulans, Crayracion fluviatilis, Dichotomycter fluviatilis, Tetraodon potamophilus, Chelonodon fluviatilis,*

Dichotomycterus rangoonensis dorsovittatus, Dichotomyterus rangoonensis.
Size: 170 mm (6 ³/₄ in).

Identifying characteristics: the coloration and markings can be variable, depending upon the fish's locality of origin. The upperside and flanks have large, round black/brown blotches with pale borders, which may unite on the back to form chevron-patterned markings. The colours of the spaces in between the chevrons are emerald green to yellow green. A pale green iridescent blotch may also be present. The underside of the fish is white, and occasionally there are dark spots present. In older specimens, the underside is grey.

The eyes have dark pupils, with a yellow/gold iris, and the nostrils have spongy tissue on the inner surface.

The fin ray count is 14 to 16 dorsal fin rays, 12 to 15 anal fin rays, and 22 pectoral fin rays. The caudal fin has several narrow bars.

The Green Puffer's coloration and markings vary according to its region of origin.

The Green Puffer can be especially aggressive towards its own species.

Natural habitat: south-east Asia, India, Burma, Sri Lanka, Bangladesh, Borneo, Philippines, Indonesia, Thailand, and the Malayan peninsula. Can be found in fresh and brackish waters. Usually found in slow-moving rivers, estuaries and the upper reaches of back-waters. Naturally occurring in shady, marginal areas.

Housing: minimum aquarium size: 36 x 15 x 12 in (90 x 38 x 30 cm).

Water: hard, neutral water conditions are required, with 10°GH and pH 7.0. The ideal temperature range is 24 to 28°C (74 to 82°F). As mentioned above, this Puffer can be found in both fresh and brackish waters, although it is best suited to a brackish environment. However, it cannot survive in full marine conditions.

Diet: omnivorous (see pages 22-24), and will accept prepared foods, such as tablet foods. This species occasionally feeds on the scales and fins of other fish.

Sexual differences: no known external sexual differences.

Breeding: the Green Puffer has been successfully bred in an aquarium, but only when kept in brackish water. When breeding, they spawn in the substrate and the male takes on the role of guarding the eggs and subsequent fry from would-be predators.

Remarks: this species is fairly common in the aquarium trade. They are active, aggressive, pugnacious fish, especially towards their own species. If kept in a community aquarium, they should be kept with fish of a similar size. The Green Puffer occupies all areas of the aquarium.

They have a tendency to inflate their bodies when excited, and care must be taken when handling them as their flesh is poisonous to both humans and animals.

RED EYE PUFFER

Also known as: no other name.
Scientific name: *Carinotetraodon lorteti.*
Synonyms: *Tetraodon lorteti, Tetraodon borneensis, Tetraodon somphongsi, Tetraodon chlupatyi, Tetraodon werneri, Carinotetraodon chlupatyi, Carinotetraodon somphongsi, Carinotetraodon lorteti, Monotreta tiranti, Monotreta caria, Tetrodan lorteti.*
Size: 60 mm (2 $^3/_8$ in).

Identifying characteristics: the body is club-shaped and somewhat compressed.

There are skin folds on the anterior part of the belly region and in the dorsal region in the males. The body coloration varies from a yellow to dark grey base colour, the dorsal lateral region of the fish is darker than the anterior region. There is a pale area between

A Red Eye Puffer (*Carinotetraodon lorteti*). The specimen pictured here has slightly overgrown teeth.

the eyes, and two irregular dark transverse stripes across the back. There is a noticeable dark band between the eye and the dorsal fin.

The underside of the fish has rust-coloured longitudinal stripes. The dorsal and anal fins are red; the caudal fin is brilliant blue with a white outer edge.

The pupils are bluish, and the irises bright red. The nostrils are very short and almost unnoticeable.

The fin ray count is 13 dorsal fin rays, 11 anal fin rays, 17 pectoral fin rays and 12 caudal fin rays. The dorsal and anal fins are short.

Natural habitat: the freshwaters of Thailand and Eastern India. Naturally found in slow-flowing or standing freshwater habitats.

Housing: minimum aquarium size: 30 x 15 x 12 in (75 x 38 x 30 cm). This fish prefers a heavily-planted aquarium with clumps of Java Moss, an open swimming space, and hiding places.

Water: hardness between 5 and 10°GH (although 5 is preferable), and a pH of 6.5. The ideal temperature range is 24 to 28°C (74 to 82°F).

Diet: carnivorous (see pages 22-24). This species can be encouraged to take tablet food once acclimatised.

Sexual differences: the male has a reddish underside to the stomach, with a red dorsal fin, which has a greyish/blue coloration at its top edge. The male's caudal fin has a white edge to it. The female has a light-grey stomach with dark spots and stripes.

Breeding: this species has been bred in an aquarium. When spawning, the male will hold the female in his jaws and up to 350 eggs can be laid in the Java Moss. The parents must be moved after spawning, as they will predate on the eggs if given the opportunity. The eggs hatch after 30 hours, but the fry are difficult to raise, and quite often perish in captivity due to starvation.

The Red Eye enjoys a heavily-planted aquarium that offers good cover.

Remarks: an active, aggressive and territorial fish, which is intolerant of most tankmates. While this Puffer likes to hide away, it will actively defend its own territory from its own species and other tank occupants. The male displays a hostile attitude towards other fish by erecting a 'comb' (part of the dorsal fin) on its back and simultaneously developing a ridge along its stomach.

These Puffers are known to change colour depending upon their surroundings, and this particular fish displays dark coloration in darker surroundings and light coloration in lighter surroundings.

The Red Eye Puffer occupies the mid to bottom ranges of the aquarium.

GIANT PUFFER

Also known as: Mbu Puffer.
Scientific name: *Tetraodon mbu.*
Synonyms: Tetrodon mbu.
Size: 750 mm (30 in).

When fully grown, this sub-adult Giant Puffer (*Tetraodon mbu*) can weigh up to 14lb (6.5kg)!

Most of the Giant Puffer's body is covered in tiny dermal spines (pictured).

Identifying characteristics: the upperside of the body and flanks, level with the pectoral fins, is yellow to orange with several dark brown/black reticulated lines. The underside of the fish is yellow. The caudal fin is orange to yellow and can have black longitudinal bands. The remaining fins are orange to yellow. Juvenile fish have large black spots instead of the reticulated lines, and also have a couple of longitudinal bands on the caudal peduncle.

This particular species has an elongated body and two forked nostrils on each side of the head. With the exception of the lower caudal region and the snout, the rest of the head and body have tiny dermal spines present.

The eyes are wide apart and are small in comparison to the rest of the body. The pupils are dark and the irises are red and gold.

The fin ray count is 11 to 12 dorsal fin rays and 10 to 11 anal fin rays.

 **Pufferfish**

Natural habitat: the freshwaters of Africa in the middle and lower Congo River. Naturally found in large rivers and lakes.

Housing: minimum aquarium size: 72 x 24 x 24 in (180 x 60 x 60 cm).

Water: medium to hard, neutral water conditions are required with 10°GH and pH 7.0. The ideal temperature range is 24 to 26°C (75 to 79°F).

Diet: carnivorous (see pages 22-23).

Sexual differences: no known external sexual differences.

Breeding: not yet known in an aquarium. As with most large Puffers, aquarium spawning is highly unlikely due to the large space required to house an adult pair.

Remarks: the Giant Puffer is perhaps the largest of the freshwater Puffers, hence its common name. It has been reported that it can weigh up to 6.5 kg or 14 lb. Only consider purchasing this species if a large aquarium can be provided. This fish is best kept as an individual specimen with other large fishes which are capable of looking after themselves (small community fish will get eaten). It occupies the mid to bottom ranges of the aquarium, and is poisonous to eat!

CONGO PUFFER

Also known as: no other name.
Scientific name: *Tetraodon miurus*.
Synonyms: Tetrodon miurus.

The Congo Puffer (*Tetraodon miurus*) has a flat neck so it can bury itself in the sand to avoid danger.

Size: 150 mm (6 in).

Identifying characteristics: this fish can camouflage itself, so there are a number of base colours that it can display – from pale grey or reddish to almost black. Its markings will also vary according to its surroundings.

The head is large and broad, with a tuberous snout. The underside of the head is flat, which makes it easier for the fish to bury itself in the sand. The eyes are relatively small in comparison to the rest of the body, and are directed upwards. The pupils are dark and the irises are reddish-coloured. The fin ray count is 9 to 10 dorsal fin rays, and 8 to 9 anal fin rays.

Natural habitat: the freshwaters of Africa, Zaire and the middle and lower Congo River. Naturally found in large rivers and occasionally in rapids.

Housing: minimum aquarium size: 36 x 15 x 12 in (90 x 38 x 30 cm).

Water: medium to hard neutral water conditions are

required, with 10°GH and pH 7.0. The ideal
temperature range is 24 to 28°C (75 to 82°F).

Diet: carnivorous (see pages 22-23). This Puffer is an
exception, as it does not feed on aquatic snails.

Sexual differences: no known external sexual
differences.

Breeding: there are no records of aquarium spawnings.

Remarks: aggressive and predatory, the Congo Puffer
should be kept on its own.
   This fish occupies the bottom range of the aquarium,
and, like the Nile Puffer (see page 44), buries itself in
sandy substrate so that it can ambush passing fish.
While in the sand, only the eyes are exposed, and the
upward-looking eyes are one of the main features of the
species.

SPOTTED GREEN PUFFER

Also known as: Spotted Puffer, Leopard Puffer.
Scientific name: *Tetraodon nigroviridis*.
Synonyms: *Tetrodon nigroviridis, Chelonodon nigroviridis,
Tetraodon fluviatilis, Tetraodon potamophilus, Tetraodon
simulans, Arothron simulans, Tetrodon simulans*.
Size: 170 mm (6 ³/₄ in).

Identifying characteristics: the base colour of the
body is green to yellowish green with large
black/brown blotches on the upper side and flanks of
the fish. The underside is white. The caudal fin has
some faint narrow bars present. The pupils are dark and
the irises gold.

The Spotted Green Puffer is also known as the Leopard Puffer because of its striking markings and temperament.

Natural habitat: Asia, Indo-China, Sri Lanka, Malaysia, Indonesia, Philippines and India. They are naturally found in freshwater streams, rivers and floodplains.

Housing: minimum aquarium size: 36 x 15 x 12 in (90 x 38 x 30 cm).

Water: hard, slightly alkaline water conditions are required with 9 to 19°GH and pH 8.0. The ideal temperature range is 24 to 28°C (75 to 82°F).

Diet: omnivorous (see pages 22-24). It will occasionally feed on the scales and fins of other fish.

Sexual differences: no known external sexual differences.

Breeding: the eggs are laid on the surface of a rock, with the male taking on the role of guarding the eggs. They can be captive-bred.

Remarks: an active and aggressive fish, especially towards its own species. If housed in a community

aquarium, they should be kept with fish of a similar size. This species occupies all areas of the aquarium.

STEINDACHNER'S PUFFER

Also known as: Topaz Puffer.
Scientific name: *Tetraodon steindachneri.*
Synonyms: *Crayracion palembangensis, Tetraodon palembangensis, Tetrodon palembangensis, Tetraodon biocellatus, Chelonodon biocellatus.*
Size: 60 mm (2 ³/₈ in).

Identifying characteristics: the underside of the body is white to yellow, while the upper side of the body is yellow and green, with irregular black blotches. An ocellus or 'eye-spot' can be seen under the dorsal fin and on the caudal peduncle, which are black with a pale border to them. There is a large black blotch on the shoulder of the fish.

The pupils are dark, and the irises are yellow to gold. The fin ray count is 9 to 16 dorsal fin rays, and 8 to 15 anal fin rays.

Natural habitat: slow-flowing or standing freshwaters of Thailand, south-east Asia, Borneo, Sumatra and Malaysian peninsula. Naturally found in freshwater environments.

Housing: minimum aquarium size: 30 x 15 x 12 in (75 x 38 x 30 cm).

Water: these fish require freshwater with soft to medium hardness, between 5 and 12°GH and pH 7.0. The ideal temperature range is 22 to 26°C (72 to 79°F).

Diet: carnivorous (see pages 22-23). Once acclimatised, they can be encouraged to eat lettuce and chopped liver.

Sexual differences: the adult female is larger and more compressed than the male.

Breeding: there appear to be no records of aquarium spawnings.

Remarks: active and aggressive, this Puffer often attacks and damages plants while foraging for aquatic snails, leaving tell-tale holes in the plant leaves. Best suited to a species-only aquarium, the fish occupies the mid to bottom ranges of the aquarium.

There are some thoughts that this fish may well be the same as *Tetraodon biocellatus* or Figure of Eight Puffer (pages 39-44). It can sometimes attain a length of 17 cm (6 ³/₄ in).

Some experts believe that the Steindachner's Puffer (*Tetraodon steindachneri*) could be the same fish as the Figure of Eight (page 39).

Measuring just one inch (2.5cm) the Dwarf Puffer certainly lives up to its name!

DWARF PUFFER

Also known as: Pygmy Puffer, Malabar Puffer.
Scientific name: *Carinotetraodon travancoricus.*
Synonyms: *Monotreta travancoricus, Tetraodon travancoricus.*
Size: 25 mm (1 in).

Identifying characteristics: as its name suggests, this is a dwarf species. The upper side of the body is yellow/brown with an irregular pattern of dark blotches. The underside is white to cream in colour. The pupils are dark and the irises gold.

Natural habitat: Asia and India (Kerala and Karnataka). Naturally found in freshwater environments.

Despite its diminutive size, the Dwarf Puffer can be aggressive with its own tankmates.

Housing: minimum size: 18 x 12 x 12 in (45 x 30 x 30 cm), which includes a substrate of good-quality aquarium sand. They prefer a brightly-lit aquarium.

Water: soft, slightly acidic conditions are preferred, with 5 to 10°GH and pH 5.8 to 6.5. The ideal temperature range is 22 to 28°C (72 to 82°F).

Diet: carnivorous (see pages 22-23).

Sexual differences: the male has a yellow coloration to the base of the caudal fin, which extends towards and below the dorsal fin. Males also have a black stripe running along their bodies.

Breeding: plant-spawners, with eggs hatching after five days at 27°C (81°F). Fry will initially feed on infusoria, Cyclops and fine Daphnia, then newly-hatched brine shrimp after a week, and larger foods as they grow.

Remarks: a very active, aggressive, fish (especially towards their own species). They are best kept in small groups to avoid aggression between themselves. They occupy all areas of the aquarium.

PERUVIAN PUFFER

Also known as: South American Puffer.
Scientific name: *Colomesus asellus*.
Synonyms: *Chelichthys asellus*.
Size: 100 mm (4 in).

Identifying characteristics: the upper half of the body is olive green with an irregular pattern of five or six dark transverse bands. The underside of the body is

The Peruvian
(*Colomesus asellus*)
is a rather peaceful
Puffer that can be
kept with other fish.

yellow to white, and the majority of the body is
covered with dermal spines.

The eyes are very mobile; the pupil is and the iris is
yellow to gold.

Natural habitat: South America: Peru, Maniti River
(near to Indiana Town), Napo River and Mazan River.
Naturally found beneath floating plants, such as Water
Lettuce and Water Hyacinth.

Housing: minimum aquarium size: 36 x 15 x 12 in
(90 x 38 x 30 cm).

Water: medium, neutral water conditions are required
with 5 to 10°GH and pH 7.0. The ideal temperature
range is 23 to 26°C (73 to 79°F).

To date, there have been no recordings of aquarium spawnings in this
species.

Sandbar in the Napo River, a tributary of the River Amazon: the natural habitat for the Peruvian Puffer.

Diet: carnivorous (see pages 22-23), taking all small live foods. Once acclimatised, they can be encouraged to eat some prepared foods, such as tablet food and sinking catfish pellets.

Sexual differences: no known external sexual differences.

Breeding: there appear to be no records of aquarium spawnings.

Remarks: peaceful and very active, this species can be quite nervous. They can show aggression towards members of their own species, but can be kept successfully with other fishes.

They are sometimes confused with the Banded Puffer (*Colomesus psittacus*), and are referred to as 'Globo' by the locals in Peru. They occupy all ranges in the aquarium.

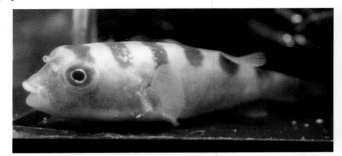

The Banded Puffer (*Colomesus psittacus*) bears a strong resemblance to the Peruvian (*Colomesus asellus*).

SUMMARY

With their unique, clumsy shape, large, expressive, eyes and ability to inflate themselves, Pufferfish have fascinated fishkeepers for many years. Owning a Puffer is very much a full-time commitment but your dedication will be rewarded many times over by watching these characterful creatures and getting to know their own unique personalities.

Puffers are rewarding, fascinating fish to keep.

DID YOU KNOW?

- Practical Fishkeeping is Britain's best-selling fishkeeping magazine.
- Practical Fishkeeping is published four weekly.
- It covers every area of the hobby for every fishkeeper from newcomer to expert.
- It covers tropical freshwater fish from community species to the rare and unusual and marine tropical fish and inverts.
- We look at ponds of all shapes and sizes from goldfish to Koi - coldwater aquarium fish.
- We publish hard-edged, in depth, up to date reviews of all the equipment you need to run a successful aquarium or pond.
- If you want to know more about the great hobby of fishkeeping it's exactly what you need.

Practical Fishkeeping
Introductory subscription offer

To subscribe to Practical Fishkeeping magazine, simply call

0845 601 1356

and quote FB11/A67 to receive 6 issues at a special price. Offer only open to UK residents. For details of overseas rates, please call **+44 (0)1858 468811.**

Practical Fishkeeping, Bretton Court, Bretton, Peterborough PE3 8DZ, Great Britain Tel: 01733 282764